Direct Ship-Side
Train-to-Steamer
Connection

HAVANA

Via Key West

$24

ROUND TRIP FROM MIAMI

10-Day Excursion Fare

The trip from Miami to Havana requires only eleven hours and has all the fascination of a trip abroad. Southbound it is entirely by daylight, including the unique experience of "Going to Sea by Rail" across the Florida Keys to Key West, thence a delightful six-hour sail on a palatial Peninsular & Occidental steamer. Leave Miami on the Havana Special 7:20 am Saturday or Wednesday, arrive Havana 6:20 pm same day. Returning leave Havana 9:00 am Monday or Thursday, arrive Miami 10:20 pm same day. This schedule permits a short week-end trip to Havana or a stay of longer duration. The $24 round-trip, 10-day excursion fare from Miami to Havana includes meals and berth on ship.

FLORIDA EAST COAST RAILWAY

in connection with

Peninsular & Occidental S. S. Co.

THE RAILROAD THAT DIED AT SEA

VISIT THE ISLAND CITY

KEY WEST

Over 100 Miles from Florida Mainland

DAILY EXCURSION	SUNDAY EXCURSION
$4.75	$2.50
round-trip	round-trip
MIAMI-KEY WEST	MIAMI-KEY WEST
in coaches	in coaches
Six-day limit	Limited to Monday

Built upon a small island over one hundred miles from the mainland of Florida, reached by the Florida East Coast Railway's marvelous Over-Sea Extension, Key West is a most unique and interesting spot. Surrounded by the sea on all sides, it possesses a quaint seafaring atmosphere and background of romantic hitory. Sponging fleets, fish docks, turtle pens, aquariums, old forts, quaint old houses, delicious sea foods, and the finest fishing to be found anywhere are among its features.

Leaving Miami 7:20 am, you arrive Key Wset 11:50 same morning. Returning train leaves 5:40 pm, arrives Miami 10:20 pm.

Train crossing Long Key Viaduct became FEC emblem

THE RAILROAD THAT DIED AT SEA

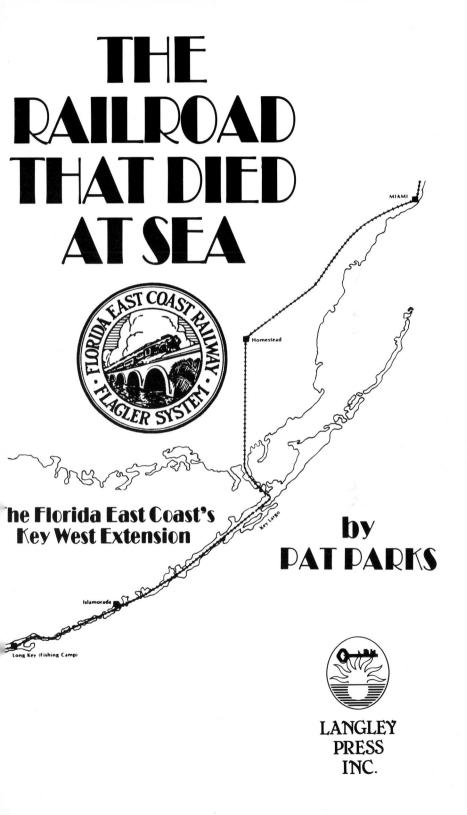

FLORIDA EAST COAST RAILWAY · FLAGLER SYSTEM

The Florida East Coast's
Key West Extension

by
PAT PARKS

MIAMI

Homestead

Key Largo

Islamorada

Long Key (Fishing Camp)

LANGLEY
PRESS
INC.

A twisted rail survives as death symbol of the
Overseas Railroad

ACKNOWLEDGMENTS

The author is grateful to the *Key West Citizen* for use
of its priceless files; to authors Frank Lovering, Nora K.
Smiley, and Louise V. White; to W.M. Lazier for loan-
ing me his copy of the last timetable of the Key West
Extension; to railroad historian Carlton J. Corliss;
to FEC officials in St. Augustine; the Henry Morrison
Flagler Museum in Palm Beach; the Key West Art and
Historical Society at Martello Tower; Harry L. Eddy of
the Association of American Railroads; Charles E.
Fisher, Railway and Locomotive Historical Society,
Inc.; to Betty Bruce and the Monroe County Library;
to Kingman Curry, Sam Drudge, Vincent McDermott,
Harold Cates, Jack Matthews, Earl Adams, and the
many other native Conchs who searched their memo-
ries for anecdotes about the railroad days. And last, a
special thanks to Wesley S. Griswold for his cheerful
aid in editing this book.

PHOTO CREDITS

Photos from FEC Railway official negatives now in the
collection of South Florida Rail Sales, 8035 Cecil St.,
Miami Beach, Florida 33141, appear on pp. 12, 15, 22
(middle), 42, 43, 44. Loaned by Eugene "Reggie"
Albury, page 31 (bottom). Courtesy of Association of
American Railroads, page 33; the Flagler Museum, pp.
38, 39, 40, 41; Florida East Coast Ry, pp. 20, 21; Florida
State University Library, frontispiece and pp. 11 (bottom), 27 (top); *Key West Citizen,* copy by Don Pinder,
page 14; the Claude C. Matlack Collection, Historical
Association of Southern Florida, pp. 5 (bottom), 19, 22
(top and bottom), 28, 31 (top), 32; Monroe County
Library Collection, copies by J.F. Brooks, 8, 11 (middle
and bottom), 13, 18, 27 (bottom); Boyce Parks, page iv;
U.S. Weather Bureau, pp. 2, 5 (top).

Printed in the United States of America, 2005.

Cover: Solares Hill Design Group

LANGLEY PRESS, INC.
821 Georgia Street
Key West, FL 33040
(305) 294-3156

FOREWORD

"Old Solomon Pinder of Knock-Em-Down Key
    Puffed on his corn cob and looked out to sea.
Word had just reached him of Flagler's great plan
    To build to Key West, the ocean to span.
'A railroad on land, that's proper,' said he.
    'But shiver my timbers! A railroad to sea!
If the story be true, sir, mark my words here:
    'Twill be a man-killer; the cost will be dear:
And many a Conch* man will go to his rest,
    E'er the first engine whistle is heard in Key West!"

—— Folksong

LIKE MANY PREDICTIONS, Old Solomon Pinder's was half right. Mile for mile, the Key West Extension of the Florida East Coast Railway, which island-hopped from the mainland tip of the state to Key West, was the most costly shortline in United States railroad history. As for killing men, its construction took several hundred workers' lives and hastened to death, through sheer strain, all the most important individuals connected with it.

Yet it was a masterpiece of railroad engineering. For twenty-three years, "many a Conch man" did thrill to the engine's whistle in Key West. Through disasters of finance, wind, and flood, the Overseas Railroad — as it was best known — kept going until it met the mightiest fury of them all.

This story begins with the fatal Labor Day hurricane of Monday, September 2, 1935 . . . the day the Key West Extension "died at sea."

Summerland Key, Florida, 1968

*Conch: anyone born in the Keys, preferably of Bahamian immigrants.

THE RAILROAD THAT DIED AT SEA

KEY WEST EXTENSION, a single-track Florida shortline that for twenty-three years defied the Atlantic Ocean, met death by hurricane on September 2, 1935. Up to that fatal day, some half-million passengers aboard its coaches and Pullmans had seldom failed to marvel over the 156-mile road.

Touted as the "railroad that goes to sea," and popularly dubbed the Overseas Railroad from its start, it skipped across twenty-nine emerald-green islands, connected by sturdy bridges and embankments. Its route lay through turquoise waters sparkling with diamond fire. From coach windows or the favored observation car, travelers on it could watch dolphins leaping from deep channels, or sharks pacing the train as it moved slowly across great bridges.

A trip on the Overseas had all the beauty of an ocean voyage without the risk of seasickness.

But on the second day of September in 1935 there were no jewel tones for the last train that left Miami for the Keys. Blue, green, and gold vistas had turned lead-grey and were being sucked into the giant centrifuge of a killer hurricane, while the engineer and his terrified crew backed steadily toward disaster at the center of it.

Along the Keys were settlers to be evacuated. At Islamorada, 90 miles from Miami, hundreds of World War I veterans working on a highway alongside the railroad awaited rescue. Their foreman that Monday had telephoned headquarters of the Florida East Coast Railway in Miami and pleaded with officials of this parent company of the Key West Extension to send a train for them. The hurricane was headed straight for their road camp.

The foreman's call was received not later than 2:35 P.M. But train-crew members, off on holiday, had to be assembled. It took almost two hours to steam up a locomotive and assemble six coaches, two baggage cars, and three boxcars. Repairs had to be made to one car before it could be used.

The train left at 4:25 P.M. It was delayed ten minutes longer by an open drawbridge, allowing passage of holiday boat traffic on the Miami River below.

At Homestead, the last mainland stop, the engineer decided to shift the powerful locomotive from front to rear of the train. It could then pull out of the storm rather than back out. This took fifteen minutes. It was now 5:15 P.M., and the hurricane was following dangerously close to the train's schedule.

At 6:50 P.M., the cars stopped at Snake Creek to take on refugees. Here a loose cable, swinging beside the track, hooked the engine cab. Men worked an hour and twenty minutes to cut it free.

By this time, winds were gusting to nearly a 200 mph cadence. Barometers were falling to 26.35, the lowest reading ever known in this hemisphere. Normal is 30.00. Waves were crashing over the track, which was only seven feet above sea level at Islamorada. The engineer, unable to see the little station through flying spray, ran several car lengths beyond it. It was 8:20 P.M. before he returned.

For five fearful minutes, men, women, and children struggled through wind and water toward the cars. Then, with a last, long sigh, the sea rose in a 17-foot tidal wave, engulfing all in a prolonged nightmare.

The hurricane's eye passed that night over the Matecumbe Keys, where Islamorada is located. By dawn, it was apparent that the islands had lived up to their somber name. Matecumbe is a corruption of the Spanish "mata hombre" — "kill man." There would be five hundred and seventy-seven bodies found, but the full total of dead was never known.

Years later, bodies in three automobiles were dug up out of a rock pit there. The cars' out-of-state licenses were all dated 1935. Skeletons are still occasionally found enmeshed in remote mangrove islands and are thought to be victims of the same savage storm.

The great wave swept the island almost clean of homes and barracks. It toppled railroad cars as if they were plastic toys. Only the 106-ton Schenectady-built 4-8-2 locomotive, "Old 447," remained upright with its tender, saving the lives of the engineer, trainmaster, and fireman.

Of the bodies that could be counted, two hundred and eighty-eight were highway workers. They met their deaths along with about three hundred Keys residents, including sixty-three members from the Russell family alone, which had numbered seventy-four and was reduced to eleven.

Some saved themselves by clinging to twisted rails of the tracks. Others splashed and swam until waters receded. Of the thousand or more persons in the area, however, more than half perished.

The sun is always hottest after a tropical storm. There was no time to bury bodies in the coral-hard Keys. For days, cremation pyres burned while survivors wept.

When news of the human tragedy was flashed to the world, it seemed almost anticlimax to announce that the Overseas Railroad had also died. Forty-two miles of filled railroad bed were washed out. Miles of railroad ties had been up-ended into a devil's jest of a picket fence. Months later, several miles of temporary track were constructed in order to salvage Old 447 valued at sixty thousand dollars.

One train marooned in Key West (scarcely touched by the storm) was eventually barged into Miami to taunting headlines of "FEC's Havana Special Arrives From Key West Months Late."

So ended the struggle of a great and visionary man who late in life

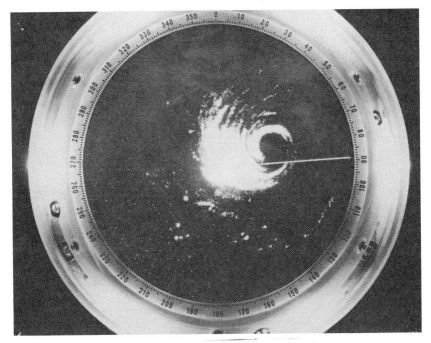

Hurricane Donna, which hit the keys in 1960, shows circular
pattern of storms which damaged the Overseas

pitted his wealth and the brilliance of young men around him against one of the most destructive forces of nature.

A severe hurricane generates an energy greater than that of an atomic bomb. It takes courage to build against such power. Yet during the twelve-year construction of the Overseas Railroad, Henry Morrison Flagler and his engineers overcame the ravages of three such storms. Gaining knowledge from these battles, they had gone ahead and in 1912 succeeded in anchoring Key West to the mainland with their iron trail. The single-track road was fully completed by 1916, and linked by ferry to Havana, Cuba.

Ground level view of the wrecked train at Islamorada

Flagler didn't live to see his railroad die. If he had, he might have resurrected it. They say he left several million from his hundred-million-dollar estate to take care of such disasters. But 1935 was a depression year. The Key West Extension had never paid its way. Officials of Flagler's FEC did not share his love for the Overseas. With cold, accountant's reasoning, they sold for $640,000 the remains of a road that had been appraised by the Federal Government at $27,280,000, and could have been repaired for $1,500,000.

No one can deny that "Flagler's Folly," as it was called, had been justified in one way. Despite the 1935 storm's crippling destruction, all of the Overseas Railroad's great concrete viaducts were still standing. They were the backbone of the line carrying trains from island to island, and they are standing today, as supports for a two-lane highway. These bridges have rebuffed enough hurricanes since 1935 to testify to Flagler's wisdom.

When the financier was asked how he could possibly build a railroad down the Keys, he replied, "It is perfectly simple. All you have to do is to build one concrete arch, and then another, and pretty soon you will find yourself in Key West."

One associate's reply to this was "Flagler, you need a guardian."

"Go to Key West"

It was in 1904 that Flagler, a tall, white-haired financier with an indomitable face, made the decisions that eventually brought the Overseas Railroad into being. One stemmed from a conference with a younger man, J. C. Meredith, who was already famous for his knowledge of reinforced concrete, a substance that the old railroad builder loved with a "passion for permanence." Meredith had just completed constructing a massive pier at Tampico for the Mexican government. Now he was being offered the most challenging job of his life, with the promise of unlimited money to back him up.

"When can you start?" asked Flagler.

"I'm ready to begin work this afternoon," replied Meredith, "but I'd like a few days first to go home to Kansas City, pack some things, and see my family. I'll have to be on this job for several years."

"All right, my boy, see your family. Then go to Key West," said the old man, confirming a rumor current since the 1890's that he would finance a railroad down the Keys.

Flagler, already seventy-five, would be gone nine years later, but not before he had triumphantly ridden his "own iron" into Key West. The young man, not so lucky, literally worked himself to death on the bold project. He collapsed April 20, 1909, five years after accepting the task of chief constructing engineer of the railroad, which would claim more than seven hundred lives before it was finished.

In 1904, news of Flagler's decision to build the road flashed across the nation. Stunned reaction was not so much "How can he do it?" as "Why would he WANT to do it?"

Key West's population was then 17,114. Between the little city and the mainland, only a few pioneer families clawed a living from what one writer in 1908 termed "worthless, chaotic fragments of coral reef, limestone, and mangrove swamps . . . aptly called the sweepings and debris the Creator hurled out to sea after He had finished shaping Florida."

These were the Florida Keys. The writer might have added that they are bounded by the Atlantic Ocean on one side, the Gulf of Mexico on the other. Between these two seas, tides surge at all times, building up to walls of brick-hard water during hurricanes.

More than one-half of the projected railroad would have to traverse bits of ocean ranging from one mile to nine miles in span, one foot to thirty feet in depth. It would cost many millions.

Flagler, son of an impoverished preacher-farmer, had those millions. While in partnership with John D. Rockefeller, he made so much money from Standard Oil that he could not possibly spend it in his lifetime. Not on his three wives, his mansions, or even the railroads that he had already pushed down the East Coast of Florida from Jacksonville to Miami.

Although Flagler retired from Standard Oil before he was fifty-three, his stock in it gushed dividends like an uncapped well until the end of his life.

Some say Flagler was always motivated by money. Others say his expenditures in Florida stemmed from a guilty conscience; that to counteract the pain of Federal investigations into questionable business practices during his time with Standard Oil, he wanted to spend the last years of his life bringing pleasure to others, using the tremendous wealth he had siphoned from the country.

Perhaps only Flagler knew his true reasons for building the Key West Extension. If he had stopped at Miami, his FEC railroads would have been money-makers. They were dotted with his luxury hotels worthy (and suggestive) of a sultan's harem, where wealthy Easterners could escape from winter cold.

Yet there were intriguing business aspects to the proposed Overseas. The War of 1898 had brought Cuba into close affiliation with the United States. Key West was only 90 miles from Havana. Flagler foresaw profit in bringing pineapples, sugar, and oranges by ferry from Cuba to Key West and shipping them by rail to New York.

The Panama Canal was about to be built. Key West would be three hundred miles closer to the "Great Ditch" than any other Gulf Port. With Flagler's railroad, the island city could become a receiving center for produce from all over the Caribbean and from Central and South America.

To build this railroad was no snap decision on Flagler's part. For several years, his agents quietly had been making surveys and estimating costs of such a road. Two years had been spent in trying to find a route through the Everglades to Cape Sable; from there over mostly open water to Key West. Miserable engineers who almost lost their lives in this survey strongly advised against the project. The mucky 'Glades, which could hardly sustain a man without sinking him hip-deep, was no place for a railroad bed.

The island-hopping route from Homestead down the Keys was considered difficult but not, like the 'Glades, impossible.

Yet when bids were called for, only one was received. Its "cost-plus" terms were not acceptable to Flagler. He decided to build the railroad himself, using men from his own company.

While consulting with his general manager and faithful follower, Joseph R. Parrott, the old man looked up from the clutter of blueprints and survey maps to say, "Joe, are you sure that railroad can be built?"

"Yes, sir, I am sure."

Then Flagler first used the phrase that throughout the hard years to come became the battle cry for his men. He said it later to Meredith; he said it to weary workers faced with rebuilding after each hurricane; he said it that day to Parrott.

"Very well, then. Go to Key West."

FLAGLER: "Joe, are you sure that railroad can be built?" ·

PARROTT: "Yes, sir, I'm sure this railroad can be built."

The First Big Test

From Homestead, on the mainland, south to 30-mile-long Key Largo, construction of the railroad was fairly simple. There was no open water to cross. But 'Glades terrain made it impossible to use mules or motor-drawn equipment.

Engineers devised two curious, shallow-draft dredges with excavators. Each dug its own canals in front of it on both sides of the center line of grade, piling dredged material behind it to form a roadbed as it moved along the surveyed line. These canals can still be seen along the present highway.

On Key Largo, the problem was labor. Three hundred Negroes from Florida and the Bahamas were used to hack out a strip through tropical jungle. The workers were made miserable by heat, mosquitoes, and stinging sand flies. Smudge fires of black mangrove did little to keep insects away. Alligators and rattlesnakes were also menaces. But at this stage, mosquitoes, more than any other factor, drove men to quitting.

Halfway through Key Largo, surveyors made an astonishing discovery. They found an inland lake a mile wide and six feet deep, with a bottom composed of peat too unstable for a trestle bridge. This body of water had not shown up on preliminary surveys, so they named it Lake Surprise. The "surprise" required fifteen months to bridge with an embankment.

Meanwhile construction camps were established along the Keys, with an advance camp on low-lying Long Key. Below this point the first great viaduct would have to be built, stretching more than two miles across open, tide-swirled water.

All along the way, the engineers were running into difficulties never before met by railroad builders. They found ready for them only the air they breathed. All building materials, food, and medical supplies for a work force running from three thousand to five thousand, had to be brought in by barge.

Fresh water alone was a tremendous problem. Of salt water there was plenty. Since there was always more liquid than land surrounding the project, it was floating stock, instead of rolling stock, that counted. Said one engineer, "It was a web-footed job all the way."

For construction, there were three tugs; thirty gasoline launches; fourteen houseboats, accommodating more than a hundred workers each; eight work boats with derricks and concrete mixers; three floating pile-drivers; one floating machine shop; and more than a hundred barges and lighters. All floating equipment was fitted with dynamos to generate electric light, for the work was such that it could not be interrupted by nightfall.

For work in shallow water, eight stern-wheel Mississippi River steamers were imported. Even these vessels, which could practically float on dew, often ran aground. One disgusted skipper bellowed that the Keys had "not quite enough water for swimming and too damned much for farming."

As for ocean-going vessels, a fleet was required. Tramp ships carried crushed rock and coal from the mainland. Others brought cement from Germany, since all concrete used below high-tide line was of this imported high-grade mix.

In January, 1906, when construction was still barely begun, the Brooklyn *Daily Eagle* estimated it would cost fifty million dollars to finish in five years. Cost in men and material soared dramatically that October to lend credence to this figure.

In order to keep on schedule, engineers decided to work through the hurricane season, which is always at its height during September and October. The advance camp on Long Key had scant weather information from Miami and Key West. Foremen depended on crude barometers made

9

from water-filled glass tubes with weeds in the bottom. They looked at these almost as often as they looked at their watches. If the pressure of surrounding air decreased, the weed would rise.

On the evening of October 17, 1906, the weed rose steadily. William H. Sanders, an eyewitness to the storm, recalled that the hurricane's full force hit early the next morning. He was chief engineer for a tugboat, and was quartered with a hundred and sixty other men on Houseboat No. 4. Only seventy-two of them survived the storm.

"By 6 A.M.," he says, "gasoline engines on all available craft were soaked and wouldn't start, so the men couldn't get to land. At 7:30, the cable broke, and our houseboat was blown southward to the Gulf Stream in a wind of more than 100 miles per hour. In Hawk's Channel, the houseboat developed leaks and planking on the sides gaped. By 9 A.M. the housing blew away. Some men couldn't swim and were afraid of sharks. They drank laudanum from first-aid kits and lay down to die."

Soon, pummeling waves separated the entire boat into loose planks. Men who survived clung to these and after the storm were picked up by freighters. Some workers ended up as far away as Liverpool, England.

The other houseboats fared almost as badly. One hundred and thirty men were known to have died, although the true count could never be certain. Much equipment was destroyed. The construction that had been started on Long Key Viaduct was damaged.

It was a staggering setback. Yet when young Meredith surveyed the ruin, he straightened his shoulders and said, "No man has any business connected with this work who can't stand grief."

Flagler simply sent word to "go ahead."

His loyal engineers tackled the clean-up work, more determined than ever to build a railroad that could withstand these merciless storms. One lesson was learned. Workers were no longer housed on boats. Wooden barracks were constructed for them on land from that time on.

A TIME OF TRUCE

The year 1907 was a time of truce in the war with the elements. With no hurricanes to divert their energies, Flagler's army of construction workers could get on with the business of building this "impossible" road.

During October, twenty-five hundred men were employed. Railroad camps had been established as far down as Knights Key, halfway to Key West. Labor was an international problem, however. The original work force used on Key Largo had proven unsatisfactory. It was replaced by men from several foreign lands. Some of the best and most trustworthy workers were Caymanders, from the islands of Grand Cayman, Little Cayman, and Cayman Brac, far out in the Caribbean. These hard-muscled, sea-faring men were at home in the climate and watery landscape of the Keys. Hundreds of Spaniards from Northwest Spain and the Minorcan Islands were brought in as common laborers. "Hard-hat" divers of Greek extraction, from the sponge beds of West Coast Florida, came with their clumsy, air-hose equipment to help the underwater work along. An occasional Norwegian turned up, but seldom stayed unless he was made foreman. The bulk of the labor force, unfortunately, had to

Above: Quarterboat, "The Duke of Donegal," housed railroad workers. Right: Time out to play Robinson Crusoe with a basket sponge for a hat. Below: A well-built mess hall at Knights Key

No. 10, one of the ancient 4–4–0s used on construction, came to FEC
from the Jacksonville, St. Augustine and Halifax line

be drawn from Skid Row and wino districts of Philadelphia and New York. Keeping these derelicts sober was a major task.

Flagler, a teetotaler, issued orders that no liquor was to be permitted in camps. But a few Key Westers with a taste for the tainted dollar found they could make big money peddling rum to isolated railroad gangs. With Conch knowledge of Keys waters, they could slip in quietly by boat with forbidden merchandise.

Soon they found they had better be wary of Flagler's foremen. If spotted, they ran the chance of facing rifle fire or of diving overboard just ahead of a stick of dynamite.

The better element of Key West tried to counteract "Booze Boats" by sending "Preacher Boats" to camps to hold services.

Lack of liquor and women created discontent. Soon the howls of unhappy Skid Row workers were heard in Washington, D.C. An investigation of Flagler's labor policies followed.

In 1907, F. S. Spofford, of the Chicago *Daily News*, reported: "Camps are clean, food good, pure ice and water supplied to each camp, no liquor sold in or near."

No foreman was permitted to carry a gun, and foremen were discharged if found brutal.

When hiring laborers from New York, FEC paid the $12 fare down, but the men had to repay this. Wages were $1.25 a day with room and board. There was free hospitalization at emergency stations in the Keys or in Miami. Workers could live well then on $2.50 per week.

Flagler and his men were eventually cleared of all charges of peonage. But so uncertain was the character of those they had to employ that the turnover remained abnormal. Although fewer than four thousand men

Forming in for the arches on two-mile Long Key Viaduct

were at work at any single time during 1907, twenty thousand had been carried down to the Keys during the first three years. Most of them had quit after their first paycheck and big drunk.

Opposition arose in another quarter. When surveys were first made for the Overseas Railroad, engineers wanted to connect all the Keys with ramparts. The U.S. Government, fearing that such a solid wall from mainland to Key West would shut off tidal flow, insisted on a certain number of bridges.

Plans were redrawn to include six miles of bridging. But this, said Keys people who knew their storms, was not enough. Concern that railroad fill would one day cause their homes to be flooded made the very people who should have been most in favor of the project quite often vociferously against it.

The native Conchs were proved right; the engineers wrong. But not until after 1907.

Despite labor dissent and local dissatisfaction, the Key West Extension forged ahead at a remarkable pace. Enough track had been laid by now so that rolling stock could be used to bring supplies from the mainland. Crossties for the rails were logs of sawed oak 10 x 12 inches square and 11 feet long. They were clamped to bridges with railroad hook bolts. The track gauge was the conventional 4 feet, 8½ inches. The rails weighed about 70 pounds to the yard.

Two of FEC's most ancient locomotives, No. 10 and No. 12, became work engines. Of the old American type (4-4-0), they had been used in mainland operations as early as the 1890's. Now these coal-burners carried all water required for the people, locomotives, and stationary steam engines of the construction job. They brought it down from Home-

13

Train of cypress tanks of fresh water, Long Key Viaduct, 1912

stead in huge cypress tanks, each holding seven thousand gallons, two tanks to a flatcar. One month's requirement was 4,500,000 gallons of water.

Much rolling stock was built on the job. This included camp cars, with sleeping and dining facilities; blacksmith-shop cars; machine-shop cars; supply cars; and a big handcar that the men called the "Bull Moose." Even the six dredges powered by gasoline engines, which Meredith had mounted on barges, were now yanked ashore, put on wheels, and slid onto a steel track when there was not enough water to float them.

About 35 miles of temporary spur tracks on wooden trestles were built to reach marl deposits, sometimes as far as a mile away from the main line. The roadbed was made of marl (a clay-like substance dredged out of the sea), riprapped with rock.

Backing up the construction engineers was Flagler's general manager, Parrott, who at one time had under charter every available freight steamer flying the American flag on the Atlantic coast. The crushed rock he ordered alone filled eighty tramps. The rest brought in 200,000 tons of coal, plus cargoes of steel, lumber, and other supplies.

The first completed triumph was Long Key Viaduct, work on which had been interrupted by the 1906 hurricane. This beautiful bridge, with its one hundred and eighty-six 35-foot reinforced concrete arches, extends over 2.15 miles of water. It required 286,000 barrels of cement, 177,000 cubic yards of crushed rock, 106,000 cubic yards of sand, 612,000 feet of piling, 5,700 tons of reinforcing rods, and 2,600,000 feet of dressed timber.

Flagler was so proud of it that a photo of a train crossing Long Key Viaduct soon became the trademark of the Key West Extension.

A Toledo, Ohio, newspaper reported, "The track is 31 feet above high water, so that passengers in the railway trains may sit in the windows of Pullman cars in serenity and have an opportunity of seeing how the Atlantic Ocean looks in a gale."

Long Key, with its sandy beaches, had been thickly planted with coconut palms. Flagler built a fishing camp there, which became famous when such notables as author-sportsman Zane Grey came via rail to spend their vacations at it. Some wealthy visitors came by boat, docking their yachts on the Gulf side of Long Key. For their convenience, Flagler built a half-mile of narrow-gauge railroad. Guests were picked up at dockside, seated on straw seats in the little cars, and taken (by way of a tunnel beneath the main Overseas line) to the Atlantic side, where cottages awaited them.

Year 1907 was a heyday of hustle and happiness for the railroad visionaries. If Long Key Viaduct had been built successfully, could not all open water between there and Key West be conquered?

The engineers did not even blanch at the thought of a nine-mile channel down the line, over which they planned to build the longest railroad bridge in the world.

"WILL FLAGLER QUIT?"

By January 22, 1908, the Overseas Railroad was a half-finished dream. One hundred and six miles had been completed. Rails from Long Key westward were joined to rails from Key Vaca eastward in time for the *Flagler Special* to run over them that same day. Knights Key, next to Key Vaca, where a Y track had been constructed, became the road's terminal for the next four years.

Key Vaca was such a beehive of activity that one worker exclaimed, "Building this railroad has become a regular marathon." The men adopted this name for Camp No. 10, located where the present town of Marathon, the Keys' second-largest, stands today.

First passenger train to make the run to Knights Key

RIDA EAST COAST RAILWAY—KEY WEST EXTENSION

Passenger Train Service Extended to Knights Key
FEBRUARY 5, 1908

VIEW OF LONG KEY VIADUCT
AND THE FIRST PASSENGER TRAIN TO MAKE THE TRIP TO KNIGHTS KEY

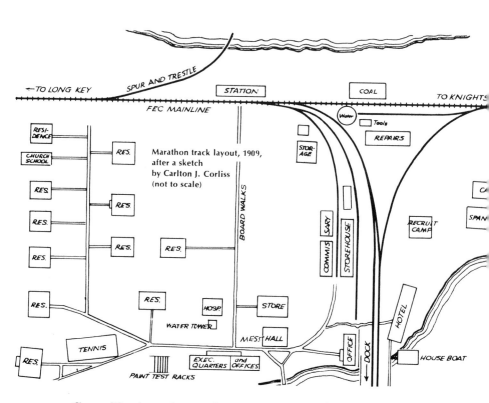

Marathon track layout, 1909, after a sketch by Carlton J. Corliss (not to scale)

Camp No. 1, made up of canvas tents, stood east of No. 10 on Pull-and-Be-Damned Creek, so named because of the difficulty of rowing or pulling a boat against the strong tide that flowed through the channel. For similar reasons, engineers dubbed the embankment across the Creek "Hell Hole Fill."

William J. Krome, principal assistant engineer to Meredith, brought his bride down to live in a Marathon cottage. The place also provided offices for engineers, barracks for workmen, recreational facilities, a hospital, shops, and power plant. All repairs to locomotives were made here.

Regular passenger service began February fifth of that year. The first timetable issued by FEC lists stations at Long Key, Grassy Key, Key Vaca, and Knights Key Dock. It does not mention Vaca, the tiniest station of all, in a lonely, jungle-surrounded part of the island. This stop was a personal victory for pioneer residents on nearby Rachel Key. They had refused to sign a quit-claim deed on that part of the right-of-way unless the mighty FEC agreed to build them a station. Once a week or more, these settlers hung out a flag, bringing the next passenger train to a full stop for their benefit alone.

About this time, word leaked out that Flagler was considering development of a great deep-water harbor at Key Vaca. Surveys and soundings to bedrock were made; maps and plans prepared that included one or more dredged channels to open sea.

A long trestle at Knights Key already carried trains to a large dock. Steamships of the Peninsular & Occidental S. S. Co. (owned by Flagler) met the trains. A brisk trade in passengers and freight built up between Knights Key and Havana, Cuba, 115 miles away. Buildings mushroomed to include the railway station and ferry terminal, customs office, post office, and a hotel boat to accommodate passengers staying overnight.

On January 4, 1909, the first through passenger train between New York and Knights Key began regular service. Called the *New York and Florida Special,* it carried standard Pullman sleeping cars on a daily (except Sunday) schedule. The *Special* left New York at 2:10 P.M., arriving at Knights Key Dock at 7:30 A.M. on the third day. The crossing to Havana took six hours.

All this achieved such a look of permanence that Key Westers became apprehensive. Rumors flew. Would Flagler quit? Would Knights Key become the important port of entry that Key West, still 50 miles away, had hoped to be?

Flagler's answer was to discard his deep-water harbor plans, while increasing his labor force and stockpile of materials. His determination to go on to Key West was so encouraging that an enraptured reporter wrote in the Key West *Citizen:*

"Key West looks northward to the fast approaching bands of steel which will bind her to the mainland and dreams of the not far distant day when she shall be a large and bustling and important city, the metropolis of the Southern Seas."

Fate had other plans for both Knights Key and Key West. On the former, nothing remains of its days of railroad glory but a few pilings and a crumbling sea wall. Key West, far from being a bustling seaport, today is a quaint little town that counts tourism, fishing, and climate as its top assets.

But during 1908 Flagler's engineers were concentrating on "the great one" . . . the Seven Mile Bridge, just below Knights Key. Preliminary work had started as early as 1906. This span, actually nine miles in length with its approaches, was proving to be the most troublesome and costly to build. In order to speed up construction, the bridge was divided into four parts.

The first three—called Knights Key Bridge, Pigeon Key Bridge, and Moser Channel bridge—consisted of steel-girder spans laid on top of concrete foundation piers. These piers were secured to bedrock, in some places 28 feet below waterline. A swinging span 253 feet long was inserted to allow free passage for boats between the Gulf and the Atlantic.

The rest of the bridge, called Pacet Channel Viaduct, consisted of two hundred and ten 53-foot concrete arches similar to those used on the famed Long Key Viaduct.

Today, motoring over Flagler's foundation, one can visualize how adventurous it must have seemed to cross this expanse of ocean by rail. At midpoint, land is almost out of sight. In the railroad's time, fire barrels of salt water were placed every few hundred feet for emergencies.

There is a curve on Pigeon Key Bridge. Some say this was to discourage train crews from building up too much speed across the monotonous span. Speed, though, was never a serious problem on the Key West Extension. Trains rarely exceeded 35-45 mph on the Keys themselves, and never crossed a bridge faster than 15 mph.

Now, though the railroad is long gone, its steel tracks remain, in a strange, upright position. When the highway was built, rails from the old Overseas were used as guard railings for the new automobile bridges.

Nineteen hundred and eight had been a year of optimism; 1909 dawned in a bustle of activity. But Flagler and his men were soon to be dealt two severe blows. The first was Meredith's death, that April. The second . . . another hurricane.

MEREDITH: "No man has any business connected with this work who can't stand grief."

KROME: "We put things through because we had to."

DOUBLE TROUBLE

Although the loss of Meredith was felt keenly by all connected with the Key West Extension, Flagler was fortunate in having William J. Krome as his second-in-command. This muscular young giant first distinguished himself in engineering at Cornell University. His work for Flagler began with the ill-fated two-year 'Glades survey, battling mosquitoes, swamps, and alligators in that first dangerous search for a route.

Since the start of the Overseas in 1904, Krome had served as first assistant to Meredith. Now, with sorrowful ease, he moved to top position. He had been devoted to Meredith, and was just as devoted to Flagler's railroad.

But the Chief was getting old. Five years had passed since he had first said, "Go to Key West." Krome was afraid that Flagler would not live to see the Extension finished. He decided to work through the hurricane season to hasten the completion of construction. Krome knew the risk he was taking. He wrote:

"No man has ever passed through one of the West Indian hurricanes and boasted that he had no fear of it. Indeed, lack of fear is dangerous. The responsibility resting upon the engineers for the safety of the men and for the preservation of equipment is heavy. There is no harbor along the entire line of the grade that is safe from hurricane. We must be ready for it when it comes; we must have the workmen well in hand to prevent panic. We must have done all we could to save our machinery and camp outfit. We have found it more economical to sink our floating equipment in the most protected waters and raise it and repair it when the storm has passed."

Remembering the great loss of life in 1906, FEC officials took extra

The curve on Pigeon Key

precautions. Telegraph wires were strung from Miami to give fast weather information. Men were quartered in strong wooden barracks. No women were allowed to remain in camp homes later than August. Transportation was held ready to evacuate all but those who volunteered to stay.

Nevertheless, when the first blow struck, in September, it was severe. Miami telegraphed to the nation that the railroad had been all but wiped out. Loss of life, always hard to tabulate in these storms, was pegged at forty.

Hurricanes are capricious and inconsistent. Perhaps that is why today each storm is given a feminine name. The unnamed vixen of 1909 played tricks on Seven Mile Bridge. It blew into the channel five deck-plate girder spans that had not yet been securely bolted into place, yet left a keg of nails perched on the bridge.

The concrete viaducts that had been completed withstood this storm with its winds of 125 mph. They had been built strong enough to buck a wind pressure four hundred per cent greater than ever recorded in the Keys. These viaducts were proving their muscle, and would continue to do so time and again. It was the filled embankments, damming hurricane tides to the breaking point, that were found to be vulnerable.

Much floating equipment was sunk. More than 40 miles of embankment and track washed out in the Upper Keys. Boulders weighing from 6 to 10 tons were rolled like pebbles into the sea. It would cost extra millions in dollars and two additional years in time to repair the damage.

Flagler still said, "Go ahead."

Krome learned two valuable lessons from this hurricane. In rebuilding washed-out embankments, he reversed the original procedure. Instead of riprapping, he now put rock inside the railroad bed, then covered all with soft, slippery marine marl. This white, mud-like substance hardens on

exposure to air. Its surface resists wave action better than rock does.

And Krome remembered the Conchs' warnings. (These stubborn island people got their nickname because of their fondness for eating the raw meat of the handsome shellfish called conchs, then using the empty shells to make horns for signalling one another at home or at sea.) The Conchs had said there were not enough bridges for free flow of water. The 1909 hurricane proved them right. Krome now put in eighteen miles of bridges where original plans had called for six.

The railroad continued to advance. It inched past Little Duck Key, Ohio and Missouri Keys (named by homesick railway workers), until it came to the mighty channel of Bahia Honda. Here, another great bridge, 5,055 feet in length with its approaches, would have to be built over the water ranging under the central spans from a minimum depth of 23 feet up to 35 feet. The Spaniards had correctly named this bay of water "Deep Bay."

Seven Mile Bridge was the most costly

Left: As a pubilicity stunt, auto rode the crossties on Long Key Viaduct, 1927, and continued all the way to Key West. Below: Temporary trestle used during construction of Knights Key portion of Seven Mile Bridge. Bottom: Swinging span for boat traffic beneath Seven Mile Bridge

It was the most water encountered so far, and it presented the greatest problems. Engineers knew that the track had to be laid above the crest of the highest hurricane wave yet recorded, so that it would not be awash during storms. Usually, the deeper the water, the higher the wave. So, above "Deep Bay" must be built a correspondingly high bridge.

As with the other bridges, both cofferdam and caisson types of construction were used for foundation piers. Cofferdams were floated into place by a catamaran and made to rest on the bottom. After all soft mud was pumped out, 24 piles for each pier were driven into bedrock as far as they could be forced. German cement that hardened underwater was piped in, forming a union with the bedrock and making the cofferdam essentially watertight.

The piling was sawed off at low-tide level. Then the form for the pier base was put in place. This, too, was filled with German cement. It took seven days to dry. Upon this foundation, each pier was built.

In preparing one such foundation for the center of Bahia Honda, workers hit a spot that was not only deep but seemed bottomless. It took a shipload of sand, gravel, and cement to fill.

The finished bridge required 13 spans 128 feet long, 13 spans 186 feet long, and 9 arches of concrete, each one 80 feet long. The arches were dovetailed at the joints with leeway left to permit expansion and contraction under heat of the intense sun. Arched steel trusses were used on top of these spans to support the railroad tracks from above.

Below Bahia Honda, the large island of Big Pine Key presented the incongruous problem of forest fires. This island is so different from the rest of the Keys that some claim it is part of the Appalachian ridge on the mainland, cut off during an ancient turmoil of the earth. It is heavily wooded with pine trees and has fresh water close to the surface, a rarity on other Keys.

Although sparsely settled during railroad days, Big Pine was a favorite for charcoal-kiln makers, burning buttonwood into fuel, and for hunters, who set fire to the land to flush out the small Key deer. These hazards, plus sparks from railroad equipment during the dry season, often set off conflagrations.

But Krome and his men were overcoming these problems. It was the hurricanes dogging their progress that hurt most. In September, 1910, another one hit.

This large storm, which lasted thirty hours, chose the Lower Keys, rather than the Upper Keys, for punishment. That, unfortunately, was where construction was concentrated at the time. Marathon was about the northernmost point above Key West to feel this hurricane's fury. Here, buildings were damaged and the railroad trestle leading to ship docks was washed away.

Below Marathon, roadbeds between the Summerland Keys, including Bahia Honda, Spanish Harbor, Big Pine, and Ramrod Keys, reverted to sea-filled channels. Tracks were washed six hundred feet west of the roadbed on Bahia Honda.

Worst blow to the engineers was the discovery that combined strength of wind and water had displaced a foundation of the center span of

Bahia Honda Bridge, the one that had required a shipload of material to anchor.

One work superintendent, caught out in the sudden storm, afterward told a nightmarish tale. He had climbed a tree and lashed himself to it with his leather belt. Only at storm's height did he realize it was a manchineel, the most poisonous tree in the tropical Keys. Some people are so allergic to the manchineel that they cannot brush against its leaves or breathe its smoke when it is burning without breaking out into a painful, dangerous rash.

Keys Indians, when fighting the Spaniards, used manchineel to poison well waters. Conquistadores developed such a fear of the "little apple," as they named it for its fruit, like the crab apple's, that one of them wrote, "He who sleeps under a manchineel sleeps forever."

The hapless foreman who accidentally lashed himself to one during the 1910 hurricane watched fearfully as his skin was gashed by rough bark and branches broken by the fierce winds. The white, rubbery toxic sap seeped into his wounds, almost costing him his life. He was many months in hospital, recovering.

Such were the torments that railroad builders endured in this lovely island chain, which soothed them with almost perfect climate most of the year, then turned on them viciously with little warning. Two hurricanes in two years. Would there never be an end to these violent storms?

"WE MUST GO FASTER"

Krome and his men had no time to brood over hurricane wreckage. Target year for completion of the Key West Extension was 1913. His health failing fast, only old Flagler's determination to ride his own road to Key West was keeping him alive. Worried associates kept after Krome.

"It was near the end of February, 1911," wrote the chief constructing engineer, "when we were asked, 'Can you finish the road down to Key West so we can put Mr. Flagler there in his private car over his own rails out of Jacksonville on his next birthday, January 2?' I did some close figuring and finally replied that we could complete the road by January 22 of that year should no storm overtake us, or no unforeseen delay set us back."

Krome kept his promise with twenty-four hours to spare.

This meant cutting a year off the schedule. To accomplish such a speed-up, work was pressed at both ends of the line. Electric lights blazed all night as dredging and filling and concrete-pouring went on without a stop. While passenger trains merrily rode the rails on the completed section from Homestead to Knights Key, final links on the remaining 50 miles were being forged by aching muscles directed by tired brains. Only a person of Flagler's caliber could have inspired his men to undertake so much in so little time.

Below Big Pine Key, there were many channels to be bridged. Although not so great in span as the "big three" (Long Key, Seven Mile, and Bahia Honda), Niles Channel Bridge is at least a mile long. Pine, Kemp, Bow, and Boca Chica viaducts are all of good size.

The large wooded islands of Cudjoe (Southern talk for "Cousin Joe") and Upper Sugarloaf offered some relief in comparatively easy track-laying. But below Sugarloaf, through the winding Saddlebunch Keys, much land was swampy and called for miles of filled embankments. From the Key West end, workers extended fill to Stock Island and laid tracks. But the task of greatest magnitude was given to J. R. Parrott, Flagler's general manager. He was made responsible for building the railroad terminal and shipping docks.

Key West is not a large island, but a town has been in existence there since 1820. Its early growth in population and wealth was a product of many trades. During its first years, Key West was a haven for pirates. These brigands used the Caribbean as their private hunting ground until 1822, when the U. S. Government asked Commodore David Porter to run them out.

Wrecking then became the most lucrative (and legitimate) trade. The Florida Keys are lined by coral reefs on the Atlantic side, which until the late 1800's were mostly unmarked by warning lights. When ships went aground during storms, Key Westers in fast sloops saved lives of passengers and crewmen, then salvaged the cargoes, reaping a large share of profits for themselves. Some old-timers remember that during the height of the wrecking days, nearly every home in Key West was furnished with rich brocades and satins, china and rugs, much of which came from wrecked ships.

Quite a few shipwrecked passengers, while waiting for transportation to take them to their original destinations, fell in love with the local hospitality, agreeable climate, or a pretty Conch girl. They never left. Today it is not unusual to meet a fourth- or fifth-generation Key Wester, descended from an ancestor who was once cast up on the Keys reefs.

When lighthouses were built, Key West lost wrecking as its chief industry, but in 1880 it became the undisputed cigar capital of the world. Thousands of Cubans fleeing Spanish tyranny settled there, and produced over one hundred million cigars a year. In addition to this enterprise, there were markets for the fine sheepswool sponge found in surrounding waters, a turtle industry, and fishing.

By 1890, Key West had become the most populous city in all Florida. Most of the island's usable land had been built upon. Present-day tourists wonder at the two- and three-story Conch homes of that era, huge dwellings built close together. With land so scarce, it was easier to build up than to spread out horizontally.

This was the situation that confronted Parrott. When he reported to Flagler that there was not enough dry land left in Key West for the Overseas terminal he visualized, his chief calmly replied, "Then make some."

Parrott did . . . 134 acres of it.

He hired Howard Trumbo as the project's head engineer. A bulkhead was thrown up around the northwest side of the island, where water was shallow. Thousands of cubic feet of mud and marl were pumped up from the bottom of the Gulf to be packed, flattened, and hardened into reliable ground. So vast was the project that U.S. Navy officials in Key West protested, claiming Parrott was digging up half the bay and using fill that the Navy might need itself someday.

Parrott debonairly replied that if this ever happened, he would return the mud. Today, Trumbo Island (as Flagler's terminal was called) is in possession of the Navy, which still uses some of the defunct railroad's buildings for training and experimental projects.

Parrott and Trumbo matched Krome's completion date of January 22, 1912. They had ready a large terminal that included a permanent pier 1,700 feet long by 134 feet wide, where steamships could dock. Trains ran right up alongside the ships, so that passengers need walk only a few feet to embark for Havana. Five to six hundred freight cars could be stored on the sidings.

On the afternoon of January 21, 1912, a bridge foreman closed the crossover span at Knights Key trestle, making it possible at last for trains to go all the way to Key West. A pilot train with a small crew left Knights Key to test the new road and found it in prime condition.

Although its arrival was marked by little fanfare, this train was officially the first to enter Key West.

THE GREAT DAY

A luminous sun shone steadily on January 22, 1912, to match the brilliant activity taking place beneath it on the Florida Keys. The *Extension Special* left Miami early that morning to carry Henry Morrison Flagler to Key West.

The engine and its tender were trailed by five passenger cars filled with notables. The last was Flagler's own private car, *Rambler*, built to his specifications in 1886 at the Jackson & Sharp plant, Wilmington, Delaware. It was luxury on rails right down to the polished brass guardrail on the observation platform.

The car was of wood construction, with a roof of copper sheeting. It was equipped with steam and signal lines and air brakes. Along the corridor from the oak-paneled lounge was Flagler's private stateroom, with its own lavatory. Across the hall was a large copper-lined shower. An open berth section provided sleeping quarters for guests, as well as dining and working space. There was a kitchen at the far end, which, though small, was equipped with icebox and a wood or coal stove. The cook slept in a bunk that dropped down from above the work counter. He needed little storage space because he could pick up fresh supplies for epicurean meals at scheduled stops.

Flagler's *Rambler*, as well as the four other cars, was filled that day with dignitaries, including the Assistant Secretary of War, as representative of President William Howard Taft. Because of the great interest in linking commercially the Key West Extension to the Panama Canal, many guests were diplomats from Latin American countries.

The Flagler Special arrives. Scene at Key West, January 22, 1912

The one bitter note was that all available space left on the first train was taken up by FEC mainland employees, from high officials to minor clerks. Anyone who had the influence to wangle an invitation did so. Krome, thanks to a last-minute telephone conversation with Flagler, was aboard. But, for the most part, hard-working engineers and bridge superintendents who had built the road, with determination, skill, and brawn, were left out.

Krome did not blame Flagler, for by this time the frail old financier was in no condition to notice the oversight. No one brought it to his attention to spoil his great day of triumph.

The trip down was enthusiastically acclaimed as a "fantastic and beautiful journey to sea." Scenic expanses of sky and ocean maintained their best tropical calm for the delightful excursion. This hurricane country had been conquered by railroading genius (or so everyone thought). The Key West Extension was proudly proclaimed to be the "Eighth Wonder of the World."

In Key West, bands played; the mayor spoke; ships in harbor blew their whistles, as the whole town indulged itself in a three-day fiesta. A chorus of school-children threw roses in Flagler's path while they sang welcoming songs. Some estimated the crowd at ten thousand that day, and a great many of the onlookers had never before seen a train.

Tears streamed down the nearly blind old man's face. "I can hear the children," he sighed, "but I cannot see them."

"I can hear the children, but I cannot see them."

To the welcoming committee, he said, "We have been trying to anchor Key West to the mainland . . . and anchor it we have done."

Flagler, too fragile for the frenzy of parties and banquets Key West had prepared, went on by ferry to Havana. Having accomplished his dream, he said, "Now I can die in peace." Less than sixteen months later, in May of 1913, Florida and the Keys lost the greatest friend they had ever had.

The importance of the Key West Extension to Flagler is underlined in a letter he wrote January 27, 1912, to J. R. Parrott, five days after his triumphal entry into Key West. His reference is to a gift of appreciation bestowed upon him that day by the men who worked under him, but also to the greater gift of the completion of Overseas Railroad while he was still living. He wrote:

"The last few days have been full of happiness to me, made so by the expression of appreciation of the people for the work I have done in Florida. A large part of this happiness is due to the gift of the employees of the Florida East Coast Railway. Their loyalty and devotion is evidenced by the beautiful gift they have sent me and for which I beg you will express to them my most sincere thanks. I greatly regret that I cannot do it to each one in person.

"The work I have been doing for many years has been largely prompted by a desire to help my fellow-men, and I hope you will let every employee of the Company know that I thank him for the gift, the spirit that prompted it, and for the sentiment therein expressed. Very truly yours, H. M. Flagler."

Service between Havana and New York was put into regular operation shortly after the celebrated entry into Key West. In August, 1912, a Havana newspaper reported:

"The all steel fast limited train service between Key West and New York via the Florida East Coast Railroad, the Atlantic Coast Line and Pennsylvania railroad in connection with the Peninsular and Occidental steamships, leaving Havana daily, except Sunday, will be resumed on Friday, August 2. This train carries the latest design all steel Pullman drawing room and Standard sleeping cars, is electrically lighted and equipped with electrical fans throughout. There is no change of cars between Key West and the Pennsylvania Station in the very heart of New York City.

"Schedule — Leave Havana, 10:30 A.M. Arrive Key West, 6:30 P.M. Leave Key West, 7:30 P.M. Arrive Jacksonville 1:55 P.M. Arrive New York, 7:55 P.M.

"Only two nights en route between Havana and New York!"

Solid gold case presented to Flagler by FEC employees on completion of the Key West Extension

Key West Extension, that casualty-prone strip of line, claimed yet another victim. Tom Jones, a worker in the railroad town of Marathon, started celebrating when he saw the Flagler special pass through at 9 A.M., January twenty-second. Seven days later Jones was pronounced dead of alcoholism.

For the most part, construction engineers, their foremen, and crews soberly set about completing the road. As passenger and freight cars thundered into full-time operation, these hard workers quietly put finishing touches to parts they had skipped over in their haste to get Flagler to Key West.

Riding a railroad to sea could be a frightening, though beautiful, experience. To allay worries of land-loving passengers, strict safety regulations were drawn up.

"There was one specific regulation," according to "Florida's Flagler" by Sidney Walter Martin, "which all who piloted trains over the Extension understood, and that was concerning cancellation of schedules in time of high wind. No train was allowed to travel over the road during times of strong wind because such pressure might sweep a moving train from the tracks, though the road itself was built to stand extremely strong wind.

"The viaducts were fitted with wind gauges which measured the velocity of the wind on every part of the great stretch of masonry and steel, and by electricity registered it at each end. This register was attached to a block system which automatically set the signal against the approaching train when the recorded wind velocity reached 50 miles per hour on any section of the bridge."

(Note: This must have interrupted train service frequently, since not only during hurricanes do great winds rake the Keys. Any wind speed over 74 mph traveling in a circular pattern, is labeled a hurricane. But since there is little land mass to act as a windbreak, the Keys, then and today, are subject to line squalls during summer electrical storms that gust to 50 mph or more. Funnel-shaped water spouts, those tornadoes spawned by the sea, though small in diameter, can overturn a heavy truck when scoring a direct hit. Tropical gales hit 60 mph; and there are winter "northers," which have been known to blow at hurricane speed but, since they come from the wrong direction and do not have the circular motion, are not called hurricanes.)

"There were many other safety precautions, one of which was the speed limit. No train was permitted to run over the bridges of the Extension faster than 15 miles per hour. Engineers said that the strength of the greatest viaducts would warrant speed of 70 mph, but the possibility of an accident from a broken rail or imperfect car equipment demanded extraordinary precautions for safety of life and property.

"Normal train speed was resumed after the viaducts were passed. With the prescribed limit of speed, half an hour was required to cross the Knights Key (Seven Mile Bridge) and almost fifteen minutes to cross Long Key Viaduct and its approaches."

Perhaps the delays for wind and the slow travel over bridges occasioned

The yard layout below, from data supplied by Capt. A. O. Sandquist, U.S.N. Ret., is superimposed on a map of Key West made after abandonment.

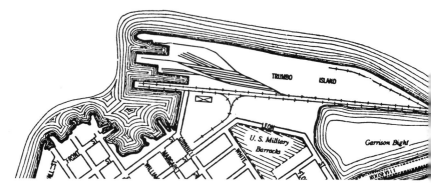

the following quip by H. H. Hyman, of Miami, an office engineer for FEC, who said, "Whenever a train was 24 hours late, it was never admitted. The bulletin board would read 'One Hour Late,' failing to state it was one day AND one hour late."

Although time schedules boasted of four and a half hours' travel time between Key West and Miami, native Conchs recall that it was usually more like six or seven hours.

The *Havana Special* was express to Miami, but the local delivered mail and merchandise at many stops along the Keys. Fishing camps sprang up at Pirate's Cove and Perky; post offices at Ramrod and Big Pine. A typical stop in those days was on Ramrod, where ice was delivered to a family pioneering on Big Torch Key. These hardy people kept a Model T Ford truck solely for the purpose of carrying the ice from the train over a short, hand-hewn road to their dock. Here they would transship it by boat to their completely water-surrounded homestead.

Pineapples were the big export from the Upper Keys. From mainland Florida to below Islamorada there was an almost continuous line of plantations for a distance of fifty-five miles. Then Cuba started growing the sweet fruit and, finding shipment easy via Flagler's ferries and freight cars, became competition hard to beat.

When the Extension was first finished, in 1912, there were no ferries, only passenger steamers. Flagler had envisioned building twelve piers at Key West, each 800 feet long and 200 feet wide. These piers were to be covered by sheds with basins 200 feet in width, each basin affording berths for four large ships. Ferries were intended to engorge not only freight cars but Pullman cars from the Overseas Railroad, so that passengers from New York need never leave their car until they set foot in Havana.

These dreams proved impractical in part, although three large steel ferries were constructed to carry freight cars. The first, the *Henry M.*

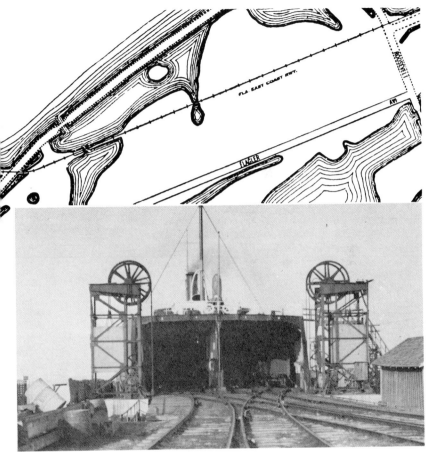

FEC tracks leading into freight car ferry

Train and boat at Trumbo Island Terminal, Key West

Flagler, was completed January 8, 1915. At the time, it was the largest car ferry in the world. It was 360 feet long, with a 57-foot beam, and was fitted out with four standard-gauge tracks. It could back right up to the dock, where, with its stern open, thirty to thirty-five loaded freight cars could be rolled aboard. These cars were held immovably in place by chocks of intricate design. Thus, by precision in distributing the rolling stock, this ferry was enabled to trim perfectly. It could make 13 knots.

Two similar ferries, the *Joseph R. Parrott* and the *Estrada Palma*, soon joined it in service.

By 1924, about thirty-five hundred carloads of pineapples passed through Key West annually. This gave employment to some two hundred men for a seasonal period of six weeks. Freight cars were fifty per cent overloaded in Havana to save space, but the fruit, which demanded ventilation and careful handling, had to be repacked for the trip to eastern cities. Arrival of a ferry was known as "Pineapple Day" in Key West. Unemployed workers flocked to the fifty-cent-an-hour task of unloading and reloading the freight. In 1926, they struck for sixty cents an hour.

All freight from Cuba was not as sweet-smelling as the "pines." On June 1, 1926, customs inspectors found three aliens (two Hungarians and one Bulgarian) sealed in with the pineapples, but far less fragrant. Worse yet, in 1927, they pulled a Bulgarian and a Jugoslavian from the big tank of a fish-oil car from Cuba on the ferry *Estrada Palma*. The aliens were half dead, besmeared and matted with smelly slime.

Freight going from Key West to Havana delighted local young boys of that era. Cuban people are fond of pork, so large aggregations of hogs were often penned up on Trumbo Island awaiting transshipment. Since Key West had no zoo (and little four-footed stock of any kind), the hogs became targets for the boys to poke sticks at. Occasionally, there were also racehorses to beguile youngsters. Seven carloads of these beauties arrived from Montreal on November 3, 1922, en route to Havana for the season's racing at Oriental Park.

Fishermen, sometimes described as "people with their brains knocked out," found special challenge in enjoying their favorite sport on the railroad's bridges. These spans were equipped with horizontal metal extensions just below the tracks to support utility lines. When an approaching train whistled a warning, fishermen on the bridges would hang from these rods, dangling over open water while passing cars made the trestles tremble.

Hand car on Long Key Viaduct. Note utility lines installation

The Overseas Railroad affected Key West's population in strange ways. Many thought the city would grow, now that rail transportation had replaced the sailboats of old. One visitor to the area found to his astonishment that more people were leaving Key West than were coming in to stay. "Now that there's an easy way out, let's go!" said quite a few islanders.

They hopped a passenger train for (they hoped) greener pastures on the mainland and a richer way of life. Many never returned, especially when the Great Depression of the 1930's began to strangle Key West's economy.

There was one "population boost" that was not wanted. During the unusually cold winter of 1932, many hoboes hitched rides on the Overseas toward the warmly desirable climate of Key West.

But before the Depression came Prohibition, when ratification of the Eighteenth Amendment became effective in 1920. Flagler, steadfastly non-alcoholic, would have been dismayed had he lived to see what a "swinging special" his New York-Key West-Havana road became for a few years.

Key West was never "closed" during the dry years. The islanders were too near to the easy Cuban source of supply. Their knowledge of secret places in twisting channels of the Keys made them accomplished rum-runners. They operated saloons in Key West equipped with false bar fronts that slid into place to hide the booze whenever a raid was staged. And they played rough with Internal Revenue agents. There were few officials with the stomach to try closing Key West.

Kingman Curry, who served as baggage master at the Key West terminal from 1915 until the 1935 hurricane blew him out of a job, recalls these days with a chuckle. Trunks of Havana returnees marked "Wearing Apparel" gurgled suspiciously when being transferred from P&O steamship to *Havana Special*. Even coffins were suspect, since quite a few Americans seemed to "die" during their Havana fling.

"I never saw a death certificate on one of those coffins that gave any other cause of death but 'alcoholism,'" Curry remembers. "It's possible some of them contained demijohns of rum. But it wasn't my duty to open them. Trunks and coffins were all sealed by customs inspectors."

Curry, who helped transfer trunks from the train to the steamship and then back again at journey's end, reports, "There was one thing I learned quickly — a lot of luggage doubled in weight and volume when people came back from Cuba."

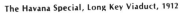
The Havana Special, Long Key Viaduct, 1912

Sometimes bags marked "clothing" sprang leaks. A baggage car of one *Havana Special* reeked of rum by the time it got to Jacksonville. Word got around that the saturated trunks belonged to an Illinois congressman on board, who had voted "dry" on the Prohibition Act.

By 1931, hard times even curbed travel on the famous *Havana Special.* There were only one arrival and one departure from Key West daily. Rates were low. Miamians could travel round-trip to Key West and Havana for $24.00. Key Westers could buy a round-trip ticket to Miami at the daily excursion rate of $4.75, or wait until Sunday and get it for $2.50.

Still, the Key West Extension performed creditably during the years from 1912 to 1935. Adhering to yet another safety regulation laid down by the Federal Government, the railroad employed divers to check underwater concrete foundations of all bridges every two years. Maintenance men walked the 156-mile road from Key West to Miami, inspecting each tie, each rail, each bolt. Wrecks were so few that accounts of them are scarce. Most were due to human error.

Meets and Other Mishaps

In 1922, an eastbound freight train crashed headlong into a westbound train carrying workers to Key West for pay day. This happened at Cross Key, 111 miles from Key West. Although both locomotives were demolished, engineers and firemen of the two saved themselves by jumping when they saw that the head-on collision was inevitable. Reports do not give the cause of the meet, but state that a flagman and two workers were killed.

One day in 1927, an engineer who was scheduled to pilot a freight carrying a hundred and ten cars of "pines" reported to the yardmaster at Trumbo Island that he was ill. Since no replacement could be found, he had to take the train out anyway. The engine's boiler was supposed to be checked at the Cudjoe Key water tank, but this was not done. On Seven Mile Bridge, near Pigeon Key, it blew up. The chassis of the locomotive was hurled into the water by the force of the explosion. The engineer was killed; the fireman badly injured.

In another wreck of the 1920's, a locomotive pulling Santa Fe cars filled with Chinese laborers was on a siding, awaiting passage of an expected freight train from the opposite direction. The freight passed. Neither engineer nor conductor of the side-tracked train made note of the engine's number or of the green flag it displayed. The signal for "second section following," it meant that another freight was coming.

The passenger train pulled out of the siding. At a curve some miles below it crashed into the second freight. Both engineer and conductor were demoted for their carelessness.

It must have been a particularly panicky wreck, though no casualties were reported. The Chinese were sealed into their cars, with windows barely cracked open, to prevent them from jumping train. Not being allowed to settle in the U.S., they were bound for Cuba to work in that country's expanding economy.

In another mishap on Seven Mile Bridge, a car suddenly dropped one of its wheel trucks. It was derailed, but the rest of the train stayed on the tracks and kept going. According to Sam Drudge, who worked in maintenance at the time, the dropped truck cut just about every bolt on the long, long bridge. When repairing the damage, workers put in two hook bolts to each tie instead of the usual one.

During its twenty-three years of operation, no passenger or freight train plunged off any of the Overseas bridges into the ocean. What wrecks there were racked up few casualties. Hurricanes brushed the Keys from time to time but caused little damage. The "railroad that goes to sea" was considered a safe one to travel.

There was only one internationally sour note about the "Eighth Wonder of the World." In 1927, a surprisingly severe winter, followed by a cool summer, plagued northern Europe. Charges were made that dredging and filling for the Overseas Railroad bed had caused a change in the path of the Gulf Stream. This mighty ocean river runs close to the Keys, passes eastern United States farther out, then curves eastward to give cold England and France the benefit of its warming waters. If Flagler had displaced their climate control, European countries wanted to know about it.

Investigations by the U.S. Hydrographic Bureau and the Weather Bureau found no reason to believe that the Key West Extension had shifted the Gulf Stream in any way.

THE DREAM ENDS

It took the Great Depression, followed by the Great Hurricane, to turn Flagler's dream into a folly. But there were other factors hastening to a lesser degree, the demise of the Overseas. Death had been, and continued to be one of them. So great had been the effort to create this 156-mile railroad that few who worked hard to build it lived long.

Flagler was an old man when he began the enterprise. But what of the young men around him? Meredith, as has already been recorded, died five years after accepting the post of chief constructing engineer. Joseph R. Parrott, who had done so much trouble-shooting and massive logistics work for the Overseas, fared little better. When Flagler died, in May, 1913, his will directed that Parrott continue as president of FEC. Parrott, that great friend of the Overseas, outlived his beloved Chief by a scant five months.

This left only Krome. He it was who had strained his heart leading the two-year survey through the trackless Everglades. He was the young giant who, after Meredith's death, pushed himself unmercifully to complete the task while Flagler was still living. When asked how he did it, he briefly replied, "We put things through because we had to."

Krome always considered his work on the Key West Extension to be his "doctorate." When the gigantic task was done, he retired to Homestead. He died there in 1932, three years before the Extension expired.

Scenes and sentiments of the Overseas from a color-printed souvenir post card folder dating from 1912

Thus the road to Key West was deprived, one by one, of its most influential friends, the men who had contributed money, brain, and brawn to the ideal of bringing it into existence.

During the Depression, the Overseas went into receivership. Those in charge had little concern for it. The line had never begun to repay its enormous initial cost or even that of its maintenance.

The $640,000 FEC received for the hurricane-wracked remains was less than the cost of one of its still-standing bridges.

There is no record of the actual amount Flagler poured into his dream. The closest estimate is from FEC files, which indicate that in 1916 the Key West Extension had a Federal valuation in round figures of $27,280,000. By comparison, the 742-mile California section of the Central Pacific, from Sacramento to Promontory, Utah, cost $23,000,000 to build. The California road clung to, or tunneled through, mountains of sheer granite, menaced by Sierra Nevada snows to depths of fifteen feet. The Key West Extension had only the sea for adversary . . . but the sea was victorious.

There is sometimes a considerable difference between the actual out-of-pocket cost of building a railroad and the valuation of it as of a given date, and even more difference between the initial cost and what the cost would be to reproduce it at a later date. Most existent accounts of the Key West Extension give it a price tag of more than $49,000,000. FEC officials today believe these higher estimates were based on replacement costs at the time the articles were written.

The Overseas Highway, now superimposed on the railroad right-of-way and bridges, remains as the greatest monument to this unique shortline.

Flagler's private car, "Rambler,"
as tenant farmer's cabin,
and (facing page) as restored for exhibition
at the Flagler Museum

REMEMBRANCE OF THINGS PAST

One further bit of glamor has been preserved. Flagler's private car, *Rambler*, in which he triumphantly rode to Key West, is a train attraction for railroad buffs visiting the Flagler Museum at Whitehall, Palm Beach. Painted a vivid yellow and brown (colors favored by the magnate for his early FEC equipment) the car now rests on lengths of rail against an immovable tropical background of palm trees.

This car, built in 1886, was in continuous service for sixty years. Flagler had it renovated in St. Augustine in 1904, then used it until his death in 1913. Although *Rambler* began to deteriorate, it remained the FEC official car until 1934, when it was sold to the Georgia Northern Railroad. In 1947 it was sold again, to the Chesapeake Western Railway, where it continued in service until 1949. *Rambler* then dropped from sight.

It wasn't until 1959 that trustees of the Henry Morrison Flagler Museum located the car, in Virginia, where it was being used as a tenant farmer's cabin. Its trucks had been removed and it rested on cement blocks. The exterior had almost totally deteriorated; its interior was a leaking shambles.

For six years, the museum trustees studied its restoration. Only in 1966, after they had located the original trucks and wheels in Tennessee, did they begin work. Now *Rambler* appears in all its earlier splendor, just as it was before the end of the 19th Century.

Since *Rambler* was usually coupled to the end of the train, its vestibule provided an unobstructed view of passing landscape. The handholds, gates, and other metal-work in the car are all original, and its signal lamps are of the vintage of 1900. There is a retaining valve marked "REDT V," which was an important safety feature on older cars. When the valve handle was pulled down, the air-brake system was activated to apply the car's brakes slightly. This prevented the weight and momentum of cars so equipped from pushing the train to an increased, and perhaps unsafe, speed on a downhill run. There is also a standard hand-brake handle, just above the rear railing.

All the paneling in *Rambler's* observation lounge is of the original oak.

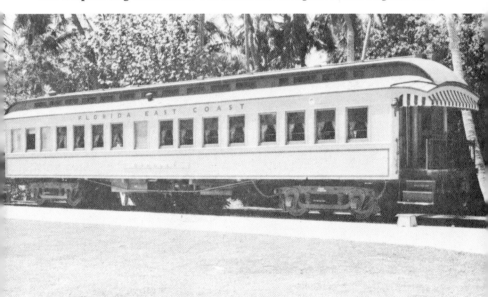

"Rambler" interiors and original trucks described in the text

The carved initials, "HMF" can be seen at either end. Original scraps of carpeting, upholstery, window shades, and draperies were sent to England to be reproduced exactly. The hand-painted ceiling has been painstakingly restored.

Brass rods projecting from overhead operated the ventilating system, a series of small windows along the clear-story, or upper deck. The signal cord is strung along the corridor.

Flagler's private stateroom was considered the ultimate in luxury in the 1880's. On the wall at the foot of the bed is a door that could be opened to permit cross-ventilation, a special comfort when traveling in Florida. The stateroom has its own lavatory with water provided, as in all such cars, from a tank located on the roof. Gravity supplemented by hand pumps furnished the meager water pressure. Later, *Rambler* was improved by the addition of a compressed-air water-pressure system. Water tanks and pumps were then attached under the car, where the pumps could be operated from the train's compressed-air line.

Most of the private cars of that era had bathtubs, but Flagler had a copper-lined shower. There was also another lavatory, across the corridor, for use of passengers occupying the open berth section. This section provided working, sleeping, and eating space for Flagler's guests and business associates. The settees and armchairs convert to beds, and above are Pullman berths screened by heavy curtains hanging from brass rods attached to the ceiling. In this section of the car there is also a heavy oak table, which could serve six.

The cook had his own private world. Although his quarters were small, they contained a sink, icebox, and wood or coal stove, as well as the previously mentioned pull-down berth. In a closet behind the stove is a Baker heater, which was patented around 1875. This device heated the car's water and radiator systems and, with a boost from the train's compressed

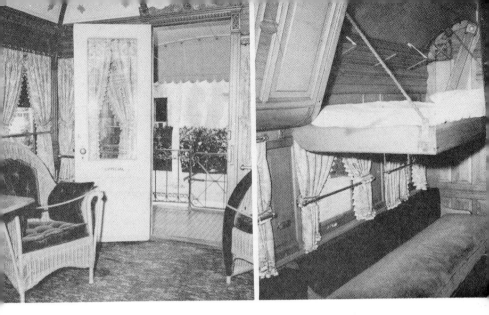

air, provided hot water for the kitchen, shower, and both lavatories as well. While the train was running, the train's steam line was used to heat the water in the heater tank. On a siding, the heater was fired with coal.

By the kitchen door leading to the vestibule is an emergency valve. A downward pull on its counter-weight would cause full application of the car's brake system.

At either end of the car are the steam and air line hose couplings. Car couplers are of the old Janney type.

Trucks of the car are unique in that they are of wood, except for the journal boxes, equalizing bar, and brake rigging. Authenticity of the trucks and wheels is born out by the date "1886" forged into the wheels. These trucks are not actually attached to the wheels, as in modern roller-bearing equipment, but ride on the axle, which juts out on both sides of the wheels. A half-round solid brass bearing rests on top of each end of the axle. The inside of the box was packed with Babbitt material to cool the journal bearing.

The air-brake system, one of the earliest types to be installed on passenger cars, is a Westinghouse model in use from 1890 to 1900. Operation is fairly simple. The cylinder marked "Air Brakes" contains a heavy spring, which is kept tightly coiled by air pressure pushing against a plunger. A quick release of the pressure by a tug on the emergency valve inside the car, or the slow release of a portion of the pressure by the engineer permits the spring to drive the plunger forward. A series of rods attached to the plunger then presses the car's shoes against the wheels.

Safety chains leading from the trucks to the body were for keeping wheels and trucks somewhere under the car in the event of a derailment. According to records, *Rambler* never had occasion to use them.

So stands the last emblem of Flagler's railroad glory . . . ready to roll but not to sea, for never again will a train whistle be heard in Key West.

No. 431 and train at Long Key Fishing Camp, a regular stop on
the Overseas as far back as 1908. This picture taken in March, 1929

LOCOMOTIVES OF THE FLORIDA EAST COAST RAILWAY, 1926

Numbers	Builder	Date	Type	Cylinders	Drivers	Weight (lbs.)
39	Schenectady	1900	4-6-0	18x24″	63″	125000
80, 96	″	1910	4-6-2	22x26″	68″	203500
151-157	″	1922	″		″	
127-136	″	1917	″	22x26″	68″	204000
141-150	Richmond	1920	″		″	
201-202	Schenectady	1907	0-6-0	20x26″	51″	146000
203-204	″	1917	″	″	″	154000
205-206	″	1920	″	″	″	157000
207-209	″	1922	″	″	″	156000
210-214	Richmond	1924	″	″	″	158000
251-253	″	1924	0-8-0	25x28″	51″	215000
256-263	″	1924	″	″	″	216000
264-267	″	1926	″		″	
268-279	″	1926	″	25x28″	51″	218000
701-715	Schenectady	1925	2-8-2	26x30″	63″	296000
301-315	Richmond	1923	4-8-2	25x28″	68″	287000
401-417	Schenectady	1924	″	26x28″	73″	313000
418	″	1924	″	″	″	318500
419	″	1924	″	″	″	313000
420-432	″	1925	″	″	″	318500
433-442	″	1925	″	″	″	322000
443-452	″	1926	″	″	″	321500
801-923	″	1926	″	28x30″	69″	356000

NOTES ON LOCOMOTIVES USED ON KEY WEST EXTENSION

Engine No. 10 — Builder: Schenectady, 1892
        CIN 3640   Type 4-4-0   Cyls. 15x22
        DD 63   sold September, 1916

Engine No. 10 was used as work engine on construction to Long Key; then was barged from Central
Supply (Long Key) to Marathon on Nov. 1907, to continue as work engine.

Engine No. 12 — Builder: Schenectady, 1892
        CIN 3930   Type 4-4-0   Cyls 15x22
        DD 63   sold May, 1914

Engine No. 12, with a caboose, formed the pilot train which tested the completed Overseas line to
Key West on the afternoon of Jan. 21, 1912, the day before the Flagler Special made its triumphant
entry. Thus No. 12 was officially the first ever to enter Key West.

Work engines No. 10 and No. 12 were two of Florida East Coast's most ancient locomotives,
having been used on mainland operations as early as the 1890's. They were of the old American type,

coal burners. They were obtained from the Jacksonville, St. Augustine and Halifax River line and the Jacksonville, St. Augustine and Indian River line when Henry Morrison Flagler's Florida East Coast absorbed these two systems. Both locomotives retained their original numbers. (This technical information obtained from Bulletin No. 86, The Railway and Locomotive Historical Society, titled "The Story of the Florida Railroads.")

Engine No. 153 — (see 1926 roster) Hauled pineapple freights from Key West to Miami.

Engine No. 447 — (see 1926 roster)
Motive power for rescue train sent to Islamorada in 1935 hurricane.

Additional information by letter from John M. Russell, Ft. Lauderdale, Fla., former chief engineer of Division 838. Brotherhood of Locomotive Engineers. Worked for Florida East Coast in 1923-24; later re-hired in winter 1936-37. Quote:

"I do know engine 153 and others of same class were on the Keys in those days. Then the 300 class came along. A Mr. William Ellis of Miami had the 308 regular on a freight run back in around 1925. He is blind, 88 years old and doesn't remember too much.

"I do know that in 1923 the engineers had regular engines with their names on the cabs and some had lodge emblems on the front of the smoke box . . . such as Shrine or Knights of Columbus.

"Mr. Ellis told me that about 1930 or 1931 after a Mr. Beals came here (to Miami) as general manager, they started running the 800 class freight engine to Key West. He (Mr. Ellis) had the first one south and when they came to Bahia Honda Bridge, the officials got off the engine, leaving himself and fireman to go over the bridge (hoping it wouldn't collapse).

Heavy mountain types like 813, above, hauled freight
on the Overseas during its last years

43

"I recall a Mr. Ben Aikin who was on a passenger run to Ft. Pierce who told me he had talked to one of the old engineers who built the railroad. (This was after the 1935 storm.) This Mr. Aikin was on a work train when the road was under construction.

"The railroad claimed (after the hurricane) it would cost four-and-one-half million to rebuild the road. The engineers said 'If we had three-fourths of a million we would soon be running trains down there again.'

"The railroad (FEC) sold the entire right of way from about a mile south of Florida City to Key West for $800.00. Of course they wanted to get rid of it as it was expensive to maintain. If they had kept it in operations until the second World War broke out and the diesel engine came along, it would have brought them out of bankruptcy.

(Note: Official selling price of remains of Key West Extension was $640,000. Eight-hundred dollars for right of way seems reasonable since State of Florida also got all rails, ties, bridges, terminals, everything except "Old 447" and the train which was stranded in Key West.)

"The water tanks I remember were at Homestead, Islamorada, Marathon, Cudjoe, and Key West. All the water was hauled from Homestead in tank cars (cypress tanks) as there was no fresh water on the Keys."

After the 1935 killer hurricane, the old pineapple freight hauler, No. 153,
gingerly pushes a survey train as far south
as possible. Note washouts near tracks

Key West & the Florida Keys

YESTERDAY'S KEY WEST by Stan Windhorn and Wright Langley. Langley Press, Inc. 144 pages. The classic pictorial history of the island city from 1821 to the 1950s. "Along with the narration, the photographs and captions [give] the reader a vigorous grasp and feel for the life and times of decades gone by."—*Update.*

Paper....ISBN 0-911607-01-3

PAPA—HEMINGWAY IN KEY WEST by Jim McLendon. Revised edition, 1990. Langley Press, Inc. 222 pages, plus 16 pages of photographs. Based on interviews with his Key West Friends, PAPA vividly recreates the people and places Hemingway came to know and love on the island. *Publishers Weekly* described the book as "an authentic picture of the birth of the Hemingway macho cult and the emergence of the 'Papa myth.'"

Paper....ISBN 0-911607-07-2

KEY WEST IMAGES OF THE PAST by Joan and Wright Langley. Images of Key West, Inc. 132 pages. Over 200 photographs and illustrations. Brief text and informative captions follow the ups and downs of the island from its purchase by John Simonton in 1821, to 1950. *Florida Keys Keynoter* called it the "natural extension of another popular history, Yesterday's Key West."

Paper....ISBN 0-9609272-0-4

Key West & the Florida Keys

YESTERDAY'S FLORIDA KEYS by Stan Windhorn and Wright Langley. Langley Press, Inc. 128 pages. A pictorial history of the Keys from their discovery by the Spanish to the 1950s. "covers many forgotten areas of the Keys both in writing and with over 200 photographs about the Keys and its people."—*Florida Keys Keynoter*.

Paper....ISBN 0-911607-00-5

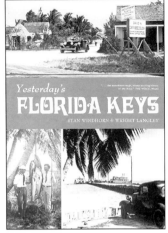

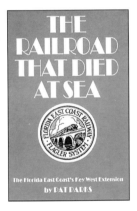

THE RAILROAD THAT DIED AT SEA The Florida East Coast's Key West Extension by Pat Parks. Langley Press, Inc. 44 pages with illustrations. The fascinating story of the construction and operation of Henry Flagler's "Overseas Railroad" that connected Key West with the maninland—until the railroad was blown away by the 1935 Labor Day Hurricane. "Not just for railroad buffs, but for readers interested in America."—*Key West Citizen*

Paper....ISBN 0-911607-05-6

KEY WEST & the SPANISH-AMERICAN WAR by Wright and Joan Langley. Langley Press, Inc. 72 pages, 66 photographs and drawings. When *Battleship Maine* blew up in Havana Harbor on February 15, 1898, Key West became the center of world attention. "...refreshing in its local and people-oriented approach, showing us the importance of the tiny island of Key West in the larger narrative of the war." —F. Lederman, GREAT PROJECTS

Paper.... ISBN 0-911607-11-0

Key West & the Florida Keys

OLD KEY WEST IN 3-D by Joan and Wright Langley. Langley Press, Inc., 64 pages. Over 50 rare stereographic views of the island dating from the 1870s to the 1920s are reproduced in duotone. Using a plastic viewer included with the book, a three-dimensional effect is achieved. Carefully researched captions explain the views; they can be enjoyed without the viewer if the reader chooses. Paper (ISBN 0-911607-04-8)